AFRICAN AMERICAN SCIENTISTS AND INVENTORS

TISH DAVIDSON

TITLES IN THIS SERIES

AFRICAN-AMERICAN ACTIVISTS

AFRICAN-AMERICAN ARTISTS

AFRICAN-AMERICAN EDUCATORS

AFRICAN-AMERICAN MUSICIANS

AFRICAN-AMERICAN SCIENTISTS AND INVENTORS

AFRICAN-AMERICAN WRITERS AND JOURNALISTS

AFRICAN AMERICANS IN BUSINESS

AFRICAN AMERICANS IN LAW AND POLITICS

AFRICAN AMERICANS IN THE MILITARY

AFRICAN AMERICANS IN RADIO, FILM, AND TV
ENTERTAINMENT

AFRICAN AMERICANS IN SPORTS

A HISTORY OF THE CIVIL RIGHTS MOVEMENT

AFRICAN AMERICAN SCIENTISTS AND INVENTORS

TISH DAVIDSON

MASON CREST
PHILADELPHIA

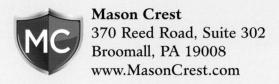

Mason Crest
370 Reed Road, Suite 302
Broomall, PA 19008
www.MasonCrest.com

Printed and bound in the United States of America.

CPSIA Compliance Information: Batch #MBC2012-5. For further information, contact Mason Crest at 1-866-MCP-Book.

First printing
1 3 5 7 9 8 6 4 2

Library of Congress Cataloging-in-Publication Data

Davidson, Tish.
  African American scientists and inventors / Tish Davidson.
      pages cm — (Major Black contributions from Emancipation to civil rights)
  Includes bibliographical references and index.
  ISBN 978-1-4222-2375-8 (hc)
  ISBN 978-1-4222-2388-8 (pb)
  1. African American scientists—Biography--Juvenile literature. 2. African American inventors—Biography—Juvenile literature. I. Title.
  Q141.D29 2012
  509.2'396073—dc23
                                    2011051942

Publisher's note: All quotations in this book are taken from original sources, and contain the spelling and grammatical inconsistencies of the original texts.

Picture credits: From the collection of The Historical Society of Oak Park and River Forest / National Science Foundation: 43; Johnson Research: 30; Library of Congress: 16, 18, 32 (right), 38; courtesy of Moorland-Spingarn Research Center: 41; National Aeronautics and Space Administration: 46, 47, 48, 49, 50, 51; images from the History of Medicine, National Institutes of Health: 11; National Library of Medicine/National Institutes of Health: 42; National Park Service: 28; © 2013 Photos.com, a division of Getty Images: 36 (bottom); used under license from Shutterstock, Inc.: 3, 7; Emin Kuliyev / Shutterstock.com: 29; Tristan Tan / Shutterstock.com: 19; photos courtesy of Thermo King: 21, 22; U.S. Patent and Trademark Office: 14, 24, 32 (left), 36 (top); Wikimedia Commons: 34; courtesy Paul Williams: 8, 10.

TABLE OF CONTENTS

INTRODUCTION

Dr. Marc Lamont Hill

It is impossible to tell the story of America without telling the story of Black Americans. From the struggle to end slavery, all the way to the election of the first Black president, the Black experience has been a window into America's own movement toward becoming a "more perfect union." Through the tragedies and triumphs of Blacks in America, we gain a more full understanding of our collective history and a richer appreciation of our collective journey. This book series, MAJOR BLACK CONTRIBUTIONS FROM EMANCIPATION TO CIVIL RIGHTS, spotlights that journey by showing the many ways that Black Americans have been a central part of our nation's development.

In this series, we are reminded that Blacks were not merely objects of history, swept up in the winds of social and political inevitability. Rather, since the end of legal slavery, Black men and women have actively fought for their own rights and freedoms. It is through their courageous efforts (along with the efforts of allies of all races) that Blacks are able to enjoy ever increasing levels of inclusion in American democracy. Through this series, we learn the names and stories of some of the most important contributors to our democracy.

But this series goes far beyond the story of slavery to freedom. The books in this series also demonstrate the various contributions of Black Americans to the nation's social, cultural, technological, and intellectual growth. While these books provide new and deeper insights into the lives and stories of familiar figures like Martin Luther King, Michael Jordan, and Oprah Winfrey, they also introduce readers to the contributions of countless heroes who have often been pushed to the margins of history. In reading this series, we are able to see that Blacks have been key contributors across every field of human endeavor.

Although this is a series about Black Americans, it is important and necessary reading for everyone. While readers of color will find enormous purpose and pride in uncovering the history of their ancestors, these books should also create similar sentiments among readers of all races and ethnicities. By understanding the rich and deep history of Blacks, a group often ignored or marginalized in history, we are reminded that everyone has a story. Everyone has a contribution. Everyone matters.

The insights of these books are necessary for creating deeper, richer, and more inclusive classrooms. More importantly, they remind us of the power and possibility of individuals of all races, places, and traditions. Such insights not only allow us to understand the past, but to create a more beautiful future.

African-American scientist Paul Williams, pictured with his wife Michelle, is a nationally recognized expert in designing computer systems that are safe from attacks by hackers.

1

BECOMING SCIENTISTS
AND INVENTORS

Growing up, Paul Williams had what looked like a typical family—a sister, a brother, and two parents. But there was one difference: the Williams children did not go to school. In 1971, when Paul was nine years old, school officials came to his house and told his parents that their children must start school. In the next three days, Paul's father sold their house and almost everything they owned.

According to Williams, his father believed that the modern world was full of wickedness and evil. To keep his children away from evil influences, he moved the family to the Ozark Mountains in Arkansas and later to an extremely isolated area on the Cumberland Plateau of south-central Tennessee. Williams says his father, "voluntarily chose a lifestyle of 'self-denial and hardship.'" To the three Williams children, this meant being cut off from children their own age, no fun or games of any kind, and many hours of hard farm work.

TEN LONG, COLD YEARS

For the next 10 years, the family lived in mountain cabins with no electricity, running water, or telephone. Williams describes the experience this way:

> Often months would pass by before we occasionally heard or sometimes saw a distant hunter. My childhood home, which was built by slaves in approximately 1860, was so dilapidated that it would snow into our home in winter, while ice would form in my bed from my breath freezing under 15 doubled-over piled up raggedy blankets. We made our own clothes and grew our own food, and we literally starved without food at times due to crop failures until my bones showed everywhere through my gaunt body and face.

The Williams children were homeschooled by their father, a former Air Force captain. Paul greedily read every book he could get about science. But his father believed that the modern world, especially computers, was evil. He had "complete intolerance for and prohibition of all things computer related."

ENTERING THE MODERN WORLD

Paul Williams left home in 1981, at age 19. For the next 11 years, he struggled to fit into society. From his reading he knew all about black holes, nuclear physics, and faraway galaxies, but he had never seen a movie or a television show. He "spoke English, but understood little of what I saw

(Top) The Williams family poses for a photos in the Ozark Mountains of Arkansas, where Paul lived in the early 1970s. (Bottom) From 1975 to 1981, Paul Williams lived with his parents and siblings in this secluded cabin in the Tennessee wilderness.

and heard around me for many years." Then, at age 30, Williams took an IQ (intelligence quotient) test. It showed that he was extremely intelligent. This knowledge helped to change him from a shy, socially uncomfortable person into an outgoing one.

Williams focused his interest on computers in part because his father had forbidden him to have anything to do with them. After taking a few classes at community college, he discovered that he was extremely good at recognizing flaws in computer security systems that other people did not see. This led him to a career as a computer scientist who finds new ways to test computer security, create secure computer networks, and fight computer crime,

A COMFORTABLE LIFE

Jane Cooke Wright and her sister Barbara grew up in a comfortable apartment in New York City. They lived in Harlem.

When they were growing up in the 1920s, Harlem was an upper-middle class neighborhood and the center of African-American culture in New York.

Education was important in the Wright family. Jane's grandfather was a doctor who graduated from Meharry Medical School and later became a minister. Jane's father, Louis T. Wright, was one of the first African Americans to graduate from Harvard Medical School. When Jane and Barbara were growing up, it was unusual for a black child to have both a grandfather and a father who had gone to college and medical school.

Jane's father was an important member of the black community. At the family dinner table, Jane often met famous African

In 1971, Dr. Jane Cooke Wright became the first woman to be elected president of the New York Cancer Society.

Americans such as actor Paul Robeson, artist Romare Beardon, and civil rights activist W. E. B. DuBois.

Jane attended exclusive private elementary and high schools. There was never any question of whether she and her sister would go to college; the only question was where they would go. Jane chose to attend the mostly white Smith College, a prestigious school for women. After she graduated from Smith, she went to New York Medical College and became a doctor.

Jane had planned to be a family doctor, but first worked for a while with her father doing cancer research at the Cancer Research Foundation at Harlem Hospital. There something happened. Jane became fascinated with finding new ways to kill cancer cells. She never became a family doctor. Instead, she became a well-known cancer research scientist.

BECOMING A SCIENTIST-INVENTOR

Paul Williams's and Jane Wright's early lives could not have been more different. The Williamses were so poor that sometimes Paul did not eat. He rarely saw people outside his own family, and he had little information about what was going on in the world. The Wright family could afford to send their children to private schools. They lived surrounded by black artists, writers, and activists. Jane personally knew some of the most famous African Americans of her time. What was it about these very different people that gave both of them the drive and ambition to become scientist-inventors?

There is no strict division between scientists and inventors. Often, scientists invent new equipment or new ways of doing things as part of their research. And inventors must study science to understand how to make new or improved tools.

All scientists and inventors share certain habits:

- They are excellent observers. They pay close attention to the world around them.
- They are curious and ask lots of questions.
- They have the self-confidence to try new things.
- They work hard and don't give up. They are willing to try and fail and try again many times before they are successful. "Failure is key to any learning, creative process," says James McLurkin, a scientist-inventor who works with robots.

Scientist-inventors also have the ambition to learn new things. Some of these inventors dropped out of school in the fifth or sixth grade, but they never stopped learning. They studied books that they borrowed from the library. They asked people on the job to teach them new skills. Sometimes they went back to school as adults. Other scientist-inventors went to college and then to graduate school where they became medical doctors or doctors of philosophy (PhD), the highest academic degree given by universities.

PROTECTING INVENTIONS

Inventors hope to make money from their inventions. The patent system used today was set up in 1836. It protects inventors from people who might steal their idea or use their inventions without permission. To

= Did You Know? =

Before the U.S. Supreme Court's Dred Scott decision in 1857, which held that people of African descent were not protected by the Constitution and could never be United States citizens, both free blacks and slaves were allowed to get patents in their own names. In the case *Dred Scott v. Sanford*, the Supreme Court ruled that African American slaves were property, not people. This meant, among other things, that they could not be granted patents. After the Civil War, African Americans were granted full citizenship and could once again patent their inventions.

How Patents are Used

People want to make money from their inventions, but they might not be able to if someone else copies their invention. To ensure that others cannot use an inventors' idea without his or her permission, the United States and many other countries have developed a patent system. Under this system, the inventor agrees to publicly disclose his or her invention. In exchange, the government will not allow others to use that invention for a certain period of time (usually 14 to 20 years). This allows the inventor to profit from his idea during that time. Once the patent expires, anyone can use the idea.

If the patent owner doesn't want to do this, he or she can charge other companies money to use their patented idea. This is called "licensing the patent." Sometimes instead of licensing the patent, the inventor will sell the patent to a company outright.

People who invent something as part of their work for a large company's research and design department usually have to sign an agreement that the patent to anything they invent at work belongs to the company and not to them. The company can then use, sell, or trade the patent.

The website of the U.S. Patent and Trademark Office, www.uspto.gov, has information to help inventors apply for patents that will enable them to make money from their ideas.

get a patent, the inventor must send the United States Patent Office a drawing of the invention and a letter explaining how it works and why it is new or improved. The patent office then searches past patents to make sure the invention is new and different. If everything is okay, a patent is issued. It gives the inventor exclusive rights to the patent for a specific time, usually 20 years. If someone wants to use the patented invention, they must pay the inventor.

People can receive patents for new or improved inventions. There are five categories of patents: process, machines, manufacture, composition of matter, and improvement. A process is a new way of doing something. A new way to make chocolate would be patented as a process. A machine is a new invention with moving parts. A kitchen mixer would be patented as a machine. An invention patented as a manufacture must be a product that does not have moving parts. Scotch tape would be patented as a manufacture. Things that are patented as composition of matter are manmade from chemicals. Paints, soaps, and medicines would be in this category. Improvements are changes to any items patented in the other four categories. For example, making an already patented paint able to withstand high temperatures would be an improvement.

Inventing is hard. Scientific research can be slow. All scientist-inventors face problems finding time and money to experiment with their inventions or do their research. African Americans have had an especially difficult time getting support for their work. The following pages tell the story of brave, intelligent, determined African Americans whose inventions and research made the world better for people of all races.

Born into slavery in 1864, George Washington Carver became one of America's greatest scientists, educators, and inventors. He discovered hundreds of different uses for crops planted by southern farmers, such as peanuts, soybeans, pecans, and sweet potatoes, helping to make those alternatives to cotton more appealing and profitable.

2

FEEDING THE HUNGRY
IMPROVING AGRICULTURE AND FOOD

People living 150 years ago could not go to the store and choose from the hundreds of different foods we have today. Back then, farmers planted small fields using only human and animal labor. There were no refrigerators or freezers to keep food fresh. There were no trucks to carry food to distant cities. People ate whatever grew near their homes. If disease or bad weather destroyed their crops, they went hungry.

Today we have many food choices. Some of these are because of discoveries made by African Americans about how to grow food, keep it safe to eat, and transport it.

A LOWLY START

George Washington Carver was a famous food scientist who became one of best-known African Americans of his time. Carver was born on a farm near Diamond Bar, Missouri, around 1864. His parents were slaves. When Carver was very young, his father died and he and his mother were kidnapped. His mother disappeared, but Carver was returned to the white family that had owned his mother.

When he was about twelve, Carver left home to get an education. He supported himself by doing chores for people who gave him food and a place to live. After graduating from high school, he went to Simpson

College in Iowa. He studied art and was a talented painter. But his real love was learning about plants, so he moved to Iowa State College to study agriculture. There he earned two college degrees.

Booker T. Washington, who founded Tuskegee Institute, a famous school for black students, hired Carver in 1896 to teach agriculture. Carver stayed at Tuskegee for the rest of his life. George Washington Carver was both a scientist and an inventor. He did research on plant diseases and on ways for farmers to grow more food.

THE PEANUT PROBLEM

In the South, people planted the same crops in the same fields every year. This used up nutrients in the soil that the plants needed to grow. As a result, over time fields became less productive. Carver introduced the idea of crop rotation—changing the type of crops planted in the same field each year. He encouraged farmers to plant peanuts every other year, because peanuts put nutrients back into the soil.

George Washington Carver (seated, center) with members of his research staff at Tuskegee Institute in the early 1900s.

Crop rotation was very successful. It helped the soil stay healthy. But it created another problem—too many peanuts. So many farmers planted peanuts that they could not sell all that they grew. Carver set out to solve this problem by finding new ways to use peanuts.

At Tuskegee, Carver invented over 270 uses for peanuts. From peanuts he created peanut butter, oil, soap, breakfast cereal, cheese, bleach, shaving cream, paper, ink, and wood stain. His work with peanuts was so important that in 1921 a group of farmers sent him to Washington, D.C., to explain the importance of the peanut to Congress. Carver took along samples of the things he had made with peanuts and impressed the legislators.

George Washington Carver was the second African American to be honored by appearing on a postage stamp. (The first was Booker T. Washington). The 3-cent stamp showing Carver's face was issued on January 5, 1948, five years after his death.

Carver also invented over 100 new uses for sweet potatoes and experimented with making dyes out of clay. He was not interested in making money from his discoveries. He only patented three of his inventions.

HONORS COME TO CARVER

Knowledge of Carver's work began to spread. He was awarded the Springarn Medal by the NAACP in 1923. In 1939 he received the Franklin Roosevelt Medal for Distinguished Research in Agricultural Chemistry. Henry Ford asked him to help develop a plastic for use in Ford cars. Famous inventor Thomas Edison offered him a job, but Carver chose to stay at Tuskegee.

George Carver never married. Plants were his passion and Tuskegee Institute was his home. He left his life savings to Tuskegee to support agricultural research. When Carver died in 1943, the *New York Times* wrote

that he had paid "no attention his clothes and refusing to make money on his discoveries, simply devoted his life to scientific agricultural research." In July 1943, the farm where Carver lived as a boy was made into a national monument. It was the first national monument dedicated to an African American and is still open to visitors today.

KEEPING FOOD SAFE

While George Washington Carver was helping people grow more food, other African Americans were finding ways to keep food fresh and safe to eat. Before electric refrigerators, people used ice to keep their food fresh. Jacob Perkins, a white man, built the first practical icebox refrigerator in 1843. John Stanard, an African American from Newark, New Jersey, improved Perkins's invention so that the icebox would keep food cool longer. Stanard patented his improvement in 1891.

Lloyd Hall found a better way to keep meat fresh. People knew that meat could be kept from spoiling by adding salt and chemicals to it. But those chemicals often made the meat taste bad. Lloyd Hall was born in 1894 and graduated with a degree in chemistry from Northwestern University in Illinois in 1914. He worked his whole life as a food chemist. His most important discovery was finding a way to put chemicals called nitrates inside salt crystals. When these crystals were added to meat, the meat stayed fresh and tasted good. He also found ways to keep food oils fresh and to make protein from plant products. By the time he died in 1971, Hall had over 100 patents. In 2004, he was inducted into the National Inventors Hall of Fame.

== Did You Know? ==

George Carver and Lloyd Hall both experienced discrimination. Carver was admitted to Highland University in Kansas based on his good grades and recommendations. However, when he showed up, he was not allowed to enter because of his skin color. Western Electric Company hired Lloyd Hall after a telephone interview. On his first day of work, he was told to leave. He could not work there because he was black.

Frederick Jones is pictured with an early refrigerator system that he developed. Jones was a prolific inventor throughout his life. His other inventions included a portable x-ray machine, a condenser microphone, a sound system and a ticket-dispensing machine for early movie theaters, and an improved two-cycle gas engine.

GETTING FOOD TO DISTANT CITIES

As America grew, more people moved away from farms and into cities. Trucks and trains brought food to the cities, but when it was hot, the food would spoil. Frederick Jones solved this problem by inventing a portable refrigerator.

Jones was born in 1893. His mother disappeared, and when he was seven, his father sent him to live with a Catholic priest in Covington, Kentucky. Two years later, his father died.

Jones did not like school. He liked taking things apart to see how they worked. And he loved cars. When he was 11, Jones dropped out of school and ran away.

His first job was cleaning up after mechanics at a garage. He learned so much about working on cars that when he was 14 that he was hired as an auto mechanic. By age 15 he was the head mechanic. Next, he started studying books to learn about electricity.

The United States entered World War I in 1917 when Jones was 24, so he joined the Army. When the Army discovered he was an excellent mechanic, they gave him the job of repairing everything from the telephone system to trucks to X-ray machines.

When the war was over, Jones went to work for Joseph Numero. Numero sold equipment to movie theaters. During this time, Jones invented a movie ticket machine and made important improvements in movie sound equipment. He also began to work on a portable refrigerator that could be used in trucks to keep food cool. In his 1949 patent application he wrote, "My device relates to a removable cooling unit for compartments of trucks, railroad cars, and the like, employed in transporting perishables."

Frederick Jones's original refrigeration systems were hung under trucks like this one.

His invention was very successful. To market Jones' invention, Jones and Numero formed a company, which is today known as the Thermo King Corporation. Jones died in 1961, but the Thermo King Corporation is still in business today, and is world-renowned for manufacturing transport temperature control systems for a variety of mobile applications, including trailers, truck bodies, buses, shipboard containers and railway cars.

HELPING DISABLED PEOPLE EAT

For most people, picking up a fork and eating is easy. For people without arms, eating is much more difficult. Bessie Blount Griffin faced this problem when she worked as a physical therapist at Bronx Hospital in New York.

Many soldiers in World War II lost their arms or were paralyzed from their injuries. They had to depend on other people to feed them. Griffin wanted to help these people be as independent as possible. She invented an electric self-feeding tube that squirted a single bite of food into the mouth each time the person bit down on the tube.

No one in the United States was interested in Griffin's electric feeder. But the government of France was interested. In 1951, she donated the patent to the French government, saying that she had proved "that a black woman can invent something for the benefit of humankind." Later Griffin patented a special basin to use in hospitals. Again no one in the United States was interested, but the basin is still used in Belgium today.

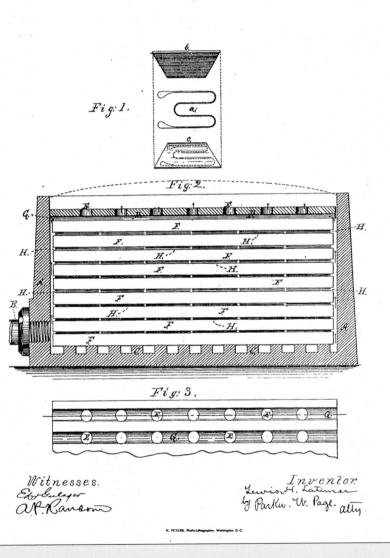

L. H. LATIMER.

PROCESS OF MANUFACTURING CARBONS.

No. 252,386.   Patented Jan. 17, 1882.

Fig. 1.

Fig. 2.

Fig. 3.

Witnesses.

Inventor.

Lewis H. Latimer

by Parker W. Page. atty.

Drawing from Lewis Latimer's 1882 patent for a better process of manufacturing the carbon filament used within a light bulb. Latimer's invention helped to make electric light affordable to ordinary Americans.

3

MAKING WORK EASIER
HOUSEHOLD
AND INDUSTRIAL INVENTIONS

Because of discrimination against people with dark skin, many African Americans were forced to work in unskilled jobs far below their abilities. They often saw ways to make these boring jobs easier or more efficient. African Americans working as servants invented improvements in the tools they used in the home. Other African Americans discovered ways to make factories faster, safer, and more efficient. Unfortunately, some of these inventors got little credit for their inventions. Others found it hard to sell their inventions when it became known that the inventors were black.

MAKING HOUSEWORK EASIER

Before there were washers, electric stoves, and vacuum cleaners, keeping a house clean and feeding the people who lived in it fed took a lot of hard work. Much of this work was done by African-American women. As they did the same chores over and over, some of them figured out ways to make their jobs easier. We do not know much about the lives of these inventors. But we do have records of the patents they got for their household inventions.

Ellen Eglin was a housekeeper in Washington, D.C., during the 1880s. She developed a special clothes wringer to squeeze water out of wet laundry. She sold her invention for $18 (equal to about $400 in 2010). She said she did this because, "you know I am black and if it was known that a Negro woman patented the invention, white ladies would not buy the wringer."

In 1892, when Sarah Boone patented her improved ironing board, there were no electric irons. Heavy metal irons were put on a stove until they got hot. Then they were used to press clothing laid out on a wide, flat board. The wide board made it hard to get the wrinkles out of shirt sleeves. Boone invented a narrow ironing board that made ironing sleeves easy. Ironing boards used today still have a narrow end for ironing sleeves.

OTHER HELPFUL INVENTIONS

Inventors were busy in the kitchen, too. In 1884, Willis Johnson of Cincinnati, Ohio, invented what he called a mechanical eggbeater. His eggbeater was really a large mixer with two bowls. This made it easy for bakers and candy makers to mix big batches of batter. Willis's eggbeater was not electric. A person had to turn a crank to make the mixer work.

Some useful inventions are very simple. In 1897, Lloyd Ray built a dustpan attached to a long handle. People could stand up and sweep trash into the pan without getting their hands dirty. The same kind of dustpan is still in use today.

Mary Kenner patented an improved toilet paper holder in 1982. Her holder keeps the loose end of the toilet paper away from the roll. This makes it easier for people who are blind or have arthritis in their hands to grasp the toilet paper.

— Did You Know? —

Between 1950 and 1990 Mary Kenner received more patents than any African-American woman. All her inventions were things that made life easier for people with disabilities. Inventing ran in her family. Her father and sister were also inventors.

A BRIGHT IDEA

Outside the home, engineers and inventors were experimenting with new ways to use electricity. In 1880,

Thomas Edison patented the electric light bulb. But Edison's bulb had problems. It was expensive to make and burned out too quickly. It took an invention by Lewis Latimer, an African American, to solve these problems. Unfortunately, Latimer was given little credit for this invention during his lifetime. Even today, his contribution to electric lighting often is overlooked.

Lewis Latimer was born in 1848 to a family of free blacks in Chelsea, Massachusetts. When he was 10

Did You Know?

Lewis Latimer's father, George Latimer, had escaped from slavery in Virginia and went to Boston, Massachusetts. Latimer's owner came to Boston to claim him and take him back to slavery. Abolitionists (people who were against slavery) raised $400 (equal to about in $9,000 today) to buy George Latimer's freedom.

years old, his father left the family. Latimer had to drop out of school and go work. At 15, he joined the U.S. Navy and fought for the Union during the Civil War.

After the war, Latimer took a job as an office boy for a group of lawyers who specialized in patents. To get a patent, an inventor needed to send in a technical drawing showing how the invention worked. The lawyers hired draftsmen to make these drawings. Lewis Latimer loved to draw. He wrote that "he watched to find out what tools were used, then he went to a second-hand book store and got a book on drawing" and taught himself. Soon he was the head draftsman. He even made the patent drawings for Alexander Graham Bell's invention of the telephone.

LATIMER LIGHTS THE WAY

Lewis Latimer understood how Thomas Edison's light bulb worked. Inside a glass bulb, electricity was sent through a thin piece of material called a filament. The filament created resistance to the flow of electricity. This resistance made the filament heat up and glow. If the filament broke, the pathway was interrupted, and the light went out. Thomas Edison used a thin carbon filament made from paper and bamboo. It was expensive to make and

Lewis Latimer (1848–1928) is best known for his work with electric lights, but during his lifetime he patented several other inventions, including an improved toilet system to be used on trains.

usually broke after a few hours of use.

Lewis Latimer set out to make a better carbon filament. After many experiments, he finally succeeded. His sturdy carbon filaments could burn for many hours and were inexpensive to make. Thanks to Lewis Latimer, ordinary working people could now afford electric lights.

Latimer sold his patent to U.S. Electric Light Company and soon went to work for that company as chief electrical engineer. He was in charge of building electric plants for cities such as New York, Philadelphia, and Montreal. In 1884 he went to London, England, to oversee building a new light bulb factory. He did a good job. But when he came back to America, he discovered he no longer had a job.

LATIMER BECOMES A PATENT EXPERT

A few years later, Latimer was hired by Thomas Edison, the most famous inventor in America. He worked for the Edison Electric Company in New York for 30 years. Latimer became a patent expert. When Thomas Edison thought other businessmen were using his patents illegally, Latimer would investigate. He often had to go to court and testify about what he had discovered. He rarely lost a case. Latimer worked for Edison until 1924. He died in 1928.

Lewis Latimer was a grade school dropout, but he invented something that improved the way ordinary people lived. He also wrote a textbook on electricity and lighting, wrote poetry, learned to read French, played the

violin, and painted. He even had a public school named after him—Lewis H. Latimer School in Brooklyn, New York.

AN ACCIDENTAL INVENTION

Lewis Latimer knew he wanted to make a better carbon filament. But some inventions are unplanned. Lonnie Johnson's accidental invention made him a millionaire.

Johnson was born in Alabama in 1949. As a kid, he liked building

Keeping People Cool

The inventions of David Crosthwait have made a lot of people comfortable. Crosthwait (1898–1976) was a heating and cooling engineer. He received 39 patents for thermostats or for improvements to heating and cooling systems. He specialized in heating very large buildings.

One of Crosthwait's biggest jobs was designing the heating system for Radio City Music Hall in New York City. The theater opened in 1932. It seated 6,000 people and needed a gigantic heating system and special inventions to make sure that audience members were neither too hot nor too cold.

Radio City Music Hall is famous for the Rockettes, a women's precision dance team. Although a black man's inventions in the 1930s kept theatergoers comfortable for many years, the Rockettes would not hire their first African-American dancer until 1988—a dozen years after David Crosthwait died.

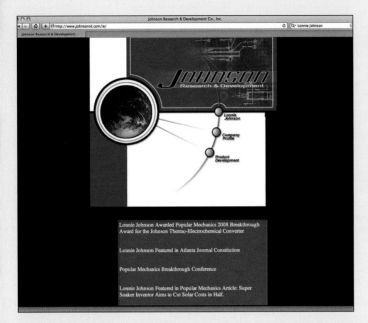

Lonnie Johnson currently owns an engineering firm, Johnson Research and Development. The company develops innovative toys and consumer products. It does not manufacture the items; instead patents are licensed to larger companies that have the sales networks and financial capacity to successfully produce, market, and distribute the items created at Johnson Research.

things. As an adult, he became an engineer, joined the Air Force, and worked for the space program. He made several technical inventions for NASA.

One day Johnson was working at home on a heat pump that could be cooled with water. He hooked a tube with a special nozzle up to the sink and turned the water on. Water blasted out of the nozzle, and the idea for the Super Soaker® squirt gun was born. The toy was a huge success and made Johnson a millionaire. Today he has his own engineering company that works on technical solutions to environmental problems.

4

GOING PLACES
TRANSPORTATION INVENTIONS

The United States is a big country. People often move far away from the places where they were born, but they still want to be able to see their relatives and visit old friends. Today people can get on an airplane and be anywhere in the country within one day. It was not always that way. Before air travel, it took several days to cross the country by train and even longer by car.

For many years, trains were the most important kind of transportation for people and freight traveling long distances. The railroads often hired black men. Some worked in the railroad yards loading freight and putting trains together. Some worked as porters taking care of the passengers. Others shoveled coal into boilers to make steam to run the engine.

Elijah McCoy was an educated engineer. Because he was black, he could only get work as a railroad laborer. But he used his intelligence to make an invention that saved time and money for the railroads and for many other industries.

THE REAL McCOY

Elijah McCoy was born in 1884. He was one of 12 children. His parents had escaped from slavery and settled in Canada. They believed education

was important, so they sent him to Scotland to study engineering when he was 15 years old. When McCoy returned to the United States, he was a master mechanic and engineer. McCoy looked for a job, but even with his education, all he could find was hard physical work.

McCoy's railroad job was to make sure the train had the right amount of steam to run the engine. It was boring work. But McCoy was clever. He noticed that the train had to stop about a dozen times a day so that the moving parts of the engine could be oiled. This was done by hand. It was a dangerous job and wasted time, but it was necessary. If the engine was not oiled, the moving parts would rub together, get too hot, and be destroyed.

E. McCOY.

Improvement in Lubricators for Steam-Engines.

No. 129,843.   Patented July 23, 1872.

Witnesses
John A. Ellis
C. H. Watson

Inventor
Elijah McCoy
by
J. H. Alexander &
Atty.

Many people tried to imitate Elijah McCoy's lubricator cup. But his was the best. Soon people buying machinery would ask salesmen if the lubricator cup was "the real McCoy." Today if something is "the real McCoy," it means that it is genuine and high quality, not a fake or imitation.

PERSISTENCE PAYS OFF

McCoy realized there needed to be a way to oil the engine automatically while the train was moving. This was a difficult problem. The right amount of oil had to get to the right parts of the engine at the right time. McCoy worked on the problem for two years. Finally, in 1872 he patented what he called a drip cup or lubricator cup for steam engines. The way it worked was explained in his patent application: "when the steam presses upon the piston the valve rises and allows the oil . . . to pass out" into the engine.

Other people had tried to make automatic lubricators before McCoy. However, his device worked so much better that even though he was a black man, railroad engineers wanted to use his invention.

McCoy was not satisfied with his first lubricator. He moved to Detroit where he continued to improve his invention. His idea could be used to lubricate machinery in factories, too. Before McCoy died in 1929, he had more than 50 patents. Almost all were for saving time and money by automatically oiling different kinds of machinery.

MAKING TRAINS SAFER

"A wreck on the tracks!" That was a common newspaper headline in the 1880s. If one train stalled, the train traveling behind it would slam into the stopped train. If a bridge was washed out, the train would fall into the river. Many people were injured or killed in these accidents. There needed to be an effective way for trains to communicate with each other and with train controllers at the stations. Telephones and telegraphs would not work with moving trains. In the 19th century, these devices needed fixed wires to send messages. Granville Woods had the answer.

Granville Woods is sometimes called the Black Edison because he had so many patents for electrical devices. Born in 1856, Woods left school at age 10. He educated himself by reading books, learning on the job, and later taking a few night school classes. His first job was in a machine shop that repaired railroad equipment. Later, like Elijah McCoy, he worked on the railroad. He also worked in a steel mill and spent two years traveling

During his lifetime, Granville Woods (1856–1910) received more than 60 patents. Most of his inventions were related to trains or street cars.

around the world as an engineer on a British ship. Everywhere he went he tried to learn as much as he could about machinery and electricity.

Woods's first patent was for a device that combined telegraph and telephone technology to send electric messages farther and make the sound clearer. He sold the patent to the Bell Telephone Company. Using electricity to send messages got Woods thinking about how trains could communicate. The key to solving the problem was an electrical property called induction.

THE INDUCTION TELEGRAPH

Electric current is made by a steam of tiny particles called "electrons" moving along a wire. If this stream is strong enough, it can cause, or induce, an electric current to flow in a second wire close to, but not touching, the first wire. Woods used this principle to create what he called the induction telegraph.

To make the induction telegraph, wire with a strong electric current running through it was installed on the ground between the train tracks. At one end of the wire was a telegraph operator in the train station. Each train had a special telegraph car. On the bottom of this car was a wire with no electricity of its own. This wire was attached to a telegraph used by the telegraph operator in the railroad car.

When the train moved, the wire under the telegraph car was only a few inches above the electrified wire on the ground. The wire on the ground induced, or made, an electric current flow in the wire on the bottom of the

telegraph car. This created a continuous electric circuit between the telegraph operator on the railroad car and the telegraph operator at the station. The operators could then send telegraph messages to each other. If a train stalled or the track was washed out, the operator could send a message so that other trains had time to stop. This helped to prevent crashes and saved many lives.

Woods developed many other electrical inventions. He found a way to power streetcars using an overhead electric wire. He also invented improvements to an electric system called the "third rail" system. The third rail is still used to power New York City subway trains.

Woods was such a successful inventor that Thomas Edison offered him a job. He turned Edison down. Woods preferred to work alone and to sell his patents to big companies. Granville Woods, one of America's greatest inventors, died in 1910.

MAKING TRAINS SAFER

In the 1880s, it was difficult to put rail cars together to form a train. The cars had to be pushed into position while a worker waited between them. The link connectors on the two cars needed to be lined up and a pin hammered through them to keep the cars together. This procedure, called coupling, was very dangerous. Many workers had their hands, arms, or legs crushed when rail cars were pushed together too fast and they couldn't get out of the way.

In 1873, a man named Eli Janney designed and patented an automatic car coupler called the Janney coupler. The device was an improvement over connecting the cars by hand, but it was not perfect. An African-American man named Andrew Jackson Beard, who lost a leg in a train yard accident, would go on to patent improvements to the Janney coupler that made joining two rail cars together much safer.

Beard (1849–1921) was born a slave on a farm in Woodland, Alabama. He grew up without any formal schooling. Freed at age 15 near the end of the Civil War, he became a farmer. While working as a farmer, Beard invented an improved plow. In 1881, he patented his design for this plow

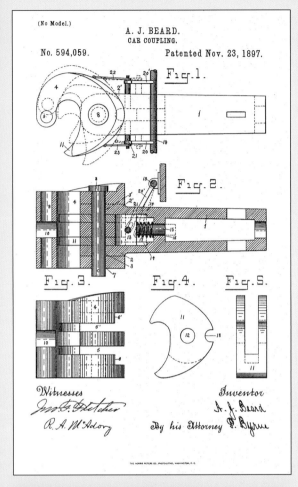

and sold the patent to a manufacturer. Six years later, he the patented another improved plow and sold it as well. The two patents made him modestly wealthy.

Beard left farming and worked at several other jobs, including on the railroad. He became interested in engines and invented a rotary steam engine that was more efficient and powerful than existing engines. He patented the engine in 1892.

While working on the design for his rotary steam engine, Beard began to experiment with the automatic car coupler for railroad cars. He made and patented improvements in Eli Janney's automatic coupler and sold the patent for $50,000 (equal to about $1.3 million today). His improved coupler is sometimes called a Jenny coupler.

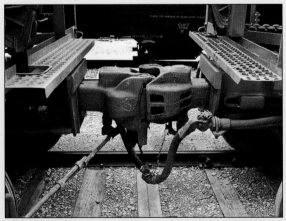

(Top) Drawings from Andrew Jackson Beard's 1897 patent application for an improved railroad car coupling system. (Bottom) The actual automatic car coupler, which was credited with preventing many accidents on the railroad. You can see a video of how the coupler works at www.youtube.com/watch?v=UANaUVybl1w.

CARS CREATE NEW PROBLEMS

Eventually cars would replace trains for long-distance travel. But in the early 1900s when the first car appeared, there were no traffic laws. Soon there were problems. At an intersection, how would people know who should stop and who should go? Garrett Morgan thought he had the answer.

The Morgan traffic signal was a pole shaped like a cross. The arms had STOP painted on one side and GO on the other. First, cars on one street would go. Then the pole would be cranked around to let cars on the other street go. When both arms of the cross were pulled all the way up, all cars stopped, and people could safely cross the street. Morgan received a patent for his traffic signal in 1923. It was used until the electric red-yellow-green traffic light we use today was invented. Garrett Morgan died in 1963.

Garrett Morgan's Gas Mask

Another of Garrett Morgan's inventions was a safety hood, or gas mask, that could filter dust, smoke, and harmful gasses out of the air. No one paid much attention to this invention until July 1916. An explosion in a tunnel in Cleveland, Ohio, trapped 32 men. Rescuers could not safely enter the tunnel because of smoke and harmful gasses in the air.

Morgan brought his gas mask to the tunnel. He put it on and went in. Some reports say he saved all the trapped men. Others say he was able to save only a few. Whichever story is true, the gas mask worked. After the tunnel explosion, fire departments and mining companies began to purchase the masks.

An African-American doctor makes a house call at a Georgia residence, circa 1900. For nearly a hundred years after the end of the Civil War, most African-American doctors were trained at the Howard University School of Medicine (founded in 1869), or at Meharry Medical College in Nashville, Tennessee (founded in 1876).

5

SAVING LIVES
ADVANCES IN MEDICINE

African Americans who wanted to become doctors faced many problems. Sometimes the schools they attended did not give them a good enough education to get into medical school. Also, medical school was expensive, and many black students were poor. Even after they became doctors, African Americans often were forbidden from working at white hospitals and treating white patients. Despite this unequal treatment, African American doctors helped to develop lifesaving procedures that would benefit people of all races.

BEATING BACK BARRIERS

Louis T. Wright went to Harvard Medical School in 1915. When it was time to learn how to deliver babies, he was told that he could not train at a white Boston hospital with the rest of his class. Louis insisted that he had paid the same tuition as the other students and should get the same training. His white classmates agreed, so Harvard permitted him to train with the rest of his class. When his training was almost over, he said that another doctor told him, "You know it's an amazing thing. You have had about 150 deliveries and there hasn't been a single complaint reach the hospital because of your color."

After being refused jobs at several Boston hospitals, Louis Wright went on to have a brilliant medical career at Harlem Hospital in New York. He specialized in treating broken bones and head injuries. He even invented a special neck brace for neck injuries. Wright had other medical interests, too. He found a safer way to vaccinate people against smallpox, and he was one of the first doctors to test new germ-killing drugs called antibiotics. Later in life he established a cancer research center at Harlem Hospital. He died in 1952 at the age of 61.

Louis Wright's two daughters, Jane and Barbara, both became doctors as well. Barbara's work helped to prevent injury, disease, and disability in workplaces. Jane became a cancer researcher. She was a pioneer in using chemicals to kill cancer cells. Today this practice is called chemotherapy. It is a standard part of cancer treatment. Jane Wright studied how to give these chemicals so that they would kill cancer cells but not healthy cells. In 1971 she became the first woman president of the New York Cancer Society. Dr. Jane Wright retired in 1987.

BLOOD IS NOT BLACK OR WHITE

Louis Wright was not the only doctor with racial problems. Charles Drew was born in 1904 in Burlington, North Carolina. He became fascinated with blood when he was a medical student in Montreal, Canada. Drew spent the rest of his life studying blood.

People have one of four different blood groups—A, B, AB, or O. Anyone can safely have a blood transfusion of their own type of blood or of type O blood. But if someone is given the wrong blood type, the blood cells clump

together and the person can die.

Doctors understood about blood types when Drew was in medical school. The problem was figuring out how to keep a supply of each type of blood ready for use. Fresh blood went bad in a few days, even when kept in a refrigerator. The red blood cells would break open and ruin the blood. If a person came to the hospital bleeding heavily, doctors had to find someone with the right blood type to donate blood. Often the person died while doctors were looking for a donor.

Charles Drew set out to find a way to keep blood fresh so that it would always be available when needed. He discovered that if blood was left standing in a container, it separated into two parts. One part was a clear yellowish liquid called plasma. The other part contained the red blood cells. Next he found that giving people just the

The pioneering work of African-American surgeon and medical researcher Charles Drew (1904–1950) has saved countless lives since the 1940s.

plasma often saved their lives. When separated from the red blood cells, plasma would keep for a week or more in a refrigerator. Later, Drew found that plasma could be dried into a powder. Plasma powder stayed good longer and could be added to special liquid when needed for a transfusion.

In 1940, Charles Drew supervised the shipment of plasma powder to Britain to save the lives of wounded soldiers fighting in World War II. Soon after that he became the first director of the American Red Cross. His job was to provide blood for American soldiers wounded in battle.

The American military issued an order that donations of blood from black people should be kept separate from white people's blood. Soldiers could receive blood only from their own race. This made Drew so angry that he resigned his job with the Red Cross and went to teach at Howard

Charles Drew teaching interns and residents during rounds at Freedmen's Hospital.

University. He told the press and the American public, "The blood of individuals may differ by blood groupings, but there is absolutely no scientific basis to indicate any difference in human blood from race to race." Today the Red Cross treats blood as just blood—not as black blood or white blood.

Charles Drew died in a car accident in 1950. The postal service issued a 35-cent stamp with his picture on it in 1981.

MAKING NEW MEDICINES

People do not have to be medical doctors to help save lives. Percy Julian was a chemist who found ways to make lifesaving medicines. Julian was born in 1899 in Montgomery, Alabama. After many years of hard work, he earned a PhD from the University of Vienna in Austria. After he returned to the United States, he taught at Howard University, but he wanted to do research. In 1936, he took a job as a director of soy research at the Glidden Company in Chicago.

Soybeans contain many useful chemicals. But they are in such small quantities that it is very expensive to get enough of them to use in manufacturing. Julian's job was to separate these chemicals, find new uses for them, and see if he could make them inexpensively in the laboratory from manmade chemicals. One of his early discoveries became a soy product called Aero-Foam. The foam stopped oil and gas fires by cutting off the fire's supply of oxygen. It was used on Navy ships during World War II and saved many lives.

Soybeans also contain very small amounts of a medically useful chemical called cortisone. Cortisone helps treat pain and swelling in the joints of people with arthritis. Cortisone was too expensive to extract from soy-

Percy Julian's work with soybeans helped to develop steroids such as cortisone, a painkiller, and progesterone, a hormone used by pregnant women.

beans for medical use. Julian studied the chemical and then found an inexpensive way to make it in the laboratory. Thanks to him, many people got relief from pain. Percy Julian died of cancer in 1975.

KEEPING THE HEART BEATING

Otis Boykin was not a doctor but an engineer. He was born in 1929. He invented improvements in electrical resistors. Resistors are put in electric circuits to help control the flow of electricity. Boykin's resistors were used in everything from household appliances to missiles. But his most lifesaving resistor was the one that was used in the first implantable heart pacemaker. A pacemaker is a device that a surgeon puts in the heart to stimulate it to beat when the heart cannot beat regularly on its own. Ironically, even though he invented an important part of this lifesaving heart device, Otis Boykin died of heart failure in 1982.

INTO THE FUTURE
AEROSPACE AND TECHNOLOGY

I
n 1961, President John F. Kennedy announced a program to put an American on the moon within ten years. Suddenly everyone was talking about the "space race." Schools began to expand their science programs. At the same time, more African Americans were going to college and earning PhDs. NASA, the American space agency, organized special programs to encourage women and minority students to get involved in space research.

In 1977, Patricia Cowings became the first African-American woman to train as a scientist-astronaut. She had a PhD in psychology and was studying why some people's bodies adjust to being in space better than others. Many astronauts vomit from motion sickness in space. Cowings wanted to find out whether training on Earth could reduce their motion sickness. Cowings trained as an astronaut for two years, but never flew a mission. She believes that her training helped better understand the problems astronauts would face in space.

A RELUCTANT FIRST

Of the 35 people chosen for astronaut training in 1978, three were African-American men. They were Guion Bluford, Ronald McNair, and Frederick

A 1978 photograph of three African Americans selected that year for astronaut training: Ronald E. McNair, Guion Bluford, and Frederick D. Gregory.

Gregory. Bluford was selected as the first African American to go into space. He was not thrilled to be the first. Twenty years after his historic 1983 flight, he said, "All of us knew that one of us would eventually step into that role. . . . I probably told people that I would probably prefer not being in that role . . . because I figured being the No. 2 guy would probably be a lot more fun."

Bluford grew up in Philadelphia and graduated from Penn State University. After graduation, he joined the Air Force. He was a fighter pilot during the Vietnam War. Later, he earned a PhD in aerospace engineering.

Bluford had plenty of fun spending 688 hours in space during four separate Space Shuttle missions. After 29 years in the Air Force, he retired with the rank of colonel. Bluford was inducted into the United States Astronaut Hall of Fame in 2010.

Guion Bluford exercises on board the space shuttle *Challenger* during his historic first flight into space, August-September 1983. He later flew three other shuttle missions.

A TRAGIC ACCIDENT

Unlike many astronauts, Ronald McNair did not have a background as a military pilot. He had a PhD in physics and was working in California when he saw an information sheet from NASA encouraging minorities to apply for astronaut training. He applied and was accepted.

McNair flew his first mission on the space shuttle in 1984. His second flight was aboard the shuttle *Challenger*. Tragically, on January 28, 1986, *Challenger* exploded soon after take off. McNair and the other crew members died instantly. At the time of his death, McNair was married and had two children.

> ═ *Did You Know?* ═
>
> In July 1967, Robert Henry Lawrence became the first African American chosen to receive astronaut training. Unfortunately, Lawrence was killed five months later during a test flight at Edwards Air Force Base in California.

OTHER AFRICAN AMERICANS IN SPACE

Frederick Gregory, the third African-American astronaut chosen in 1978, is the nephew of blood bank innovator Charles Drew. He had graduated from the Air Force Academy and served in Vietnam and as a test pilot before being selected as an NASA astronaut.

Gregory flew three successful space shuttle missions. In May 1985, he became the first African American to pilot the space shuttle. His next mission, in November 1989, he was the first African-American shuttle commander. Gregory also commanded the shuttle on its November-December 1991 mission.

After his third mission, Gregory continued to work at NASA as an administrator. He first worked in the Office of Safety and Mission Assurance from 1992 to 2001, then was

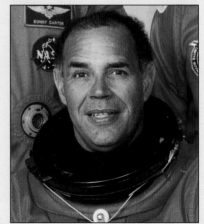

Frederick Drew Gregory

(Top) The crew of the space shuttle *Challenger* for its January 1986 mission included (front, left to right) Mike Smith, Mission Commander Dick Scobee, Ron McNair, (back) Ellison S. Onizuka, civilian teacher Christa McAuliffe, Greg Jarvis, and Judith Resnik. All were killed when *Challenger* exploded (bottom left) 104 seconds after takeoff on January 28, 1986. (Bottom right) Icicles hang from *Challenger*'s launch pad several hours before the fateful shuttle launch. An investigation determined that unexpectedly cold weather on the morning of the launch had caused a rubber gasket called an O-ring to fail, leading to the explosion.

appointed associate administrator for the Office of Space Flight (2001-2002) and NASA Deputy Administrator (2002-2005). In early 2005, Gregory served briefly as NASA's Acting Administrator. Frederick Gregory resigned from NASA in October 2005.

A BLACK WOMAN IN SPACE

Nine years after Guion Bluford became the first African-American man in space, Mae Jemison became the first African-American woman in space. Jemison was a medical doctor. At age 26, she went to Africa with the Peace

Scientists Behind the Astronauts

Astronauts are the public face of NASA, but many other scientists work behind the scenes to make space flights possible. A few of the African Americans who contributed to the success of the space program include:

- Evelyn Boyd Granville was one of the first African-American women to get a PhD in mathematics. One of her jobs was to calculate the correct orbits for NASA spacecrafts.

- Aprille Ericcson was an aeronautical engineer. Her job at NASA involved doing computer simulations to help design spacecraft that would remain stable and not spin wildly in space.

- George Carruthers designed a special camera to detect ultraviolet radiation in space. His camera was used on the Apollo 16 mission to the moon. He is pictured explaining his camera to the Apollo 16 commander, John Young.

Dr. Patricia Cowings (left) was the first African-American woman chosen for astronaut training, in 1977. Although she never flew in space, she continued to work as a NASA scientist for 30 years. Her work on the effects of zero gravity helped many astronauts, including Dr. Mae Jemison (right), who in 1992 became the first African-American woman in space.

Corps. Still, she had always wanted to go into space, and applied for astronaut training. In 1992, she flew on the space shuttle *Endeavor*. Of her flight she said,

> Since I was a little girl I had always assumed I would go into space. When I grew up in the 1960s, the only American astronauts were men. Looking out the window of that space shuttle, I thought if that little girl growing up in Chicago could see her older self now, she would have a huge grin on her face.

Mae Jemison left NASA in 1993 to start her own company. It makes devices to monitor people's stress and other physical conditions.

THE NEW WORLD OF COMPUTERS

When people in the 1960s thought about the future, they thought of space exploration and computers. Today space exploration still seems like something futuristic that is available to only a few people. But computers have become a part of everyday life.

During the 1970s computers were big, expensive machines called mainframes. Only the government, universities, and big businesses could afford a computer. In the early 1980s, though, computers became smaller and

inexpensive enough that regular people could buy them. Mark Dean, an African-American computer scientist, helped make the personal computer revolution possible.

Mark Dean was born in Jefferson City, Tennessee. He was always a good student. He was so good, in fact, that he remembers a white student asking him if he was sure he was black because he was so smart. Dean graduated from college with a degree in electrical engineering. He went back to school later in life and earned a PhD from Stanford University.

Dean worked at IBM in a group that was developing the personal computer. With co-inventor Dennis Moeller, he developed what is called the Industry Standard Architecture (ISA) bus. In computer terms, a bus is a subsystem that transfers data between components inside a computer, or between computers. The ISA bus allows keyboards and printers to be plugged into a personal computer.

In 1995 Mark Dean was made an IBM Fellow. At that time there were only 50 IBM Fellows in a company with 300,000 employees. As a Fellow, Dean was free to investigate ideas that interested him. He now has more than 40 patents.

THE ROBOTS ARE COMING

Inventions that have allowed computers to shrink in size and increase in power allow computer scientists like James McLurkin to play with robots— lots of robots.

McLurkin was born in 1972. He grew up on Long Island where he says, "I don't remember a time when I wasn't building something." Although he was a good student, school was not always fun. "Being Black and intelligent in high school in America is a very difficult thing to do. I was a geek . . . and didn't quite fit in," he later said. McLurkin went to Massachusetts Institute of Technology. At MIT he felt at home among other highly intelligent people. He eventually earned a PhD.

McLurkin is now a university professor. His goal is to program 1,000 robots so that they can share information and work together to do a job without additional directions from humans. He calls these robots swarms.